Lessons from the Incline

Thirty-one Applications to Life, Business and Goal Achievement

Jamie Efaw

CONTENTS

DEDICATION

This book is dedicated to anyone who has ever climbed the Manitou Incline—whether you've done it fast or slow, one time or over one thousand times. You are the inspiration for this book. This especially includes my friend and regular Incline hiker, John Bittner.

ACKNOWLEDGMENT

Since this is self-published book, I had no agent or editor. Instead, my parents, Jim & Susan Efaw served as my primary readers and editors. Thanks Mom & Dad.

FOREWORD

Jamie had some reasons for asking me to write the foreword to this book.

These reasons are good, However, my reasons for agreeing are different: I studied literature at university, wrote a memoir once upon a time, and most importantly writing this foreword would be a significant challenge for me.

Voluntarily taking on challenges, pursuing goals; this is Good. This is what the book is about. Whether it be marching up a mountainside or otherwise. It is You who decided to do so, and that makes it worthy. And you never know who might be inspired as a result. In fact, that's how, after reading his book, I found myself standing next to Jamie at the base of the Manitou Incline. However, this is not the first time we have met.

We first met at Dartmouth College. We had both self-selected into a program that would improve ourselves, but we were also sending a message that we were near completion of an immense stage in our lives. And even though we have this in common, there are certainly some differences. At the time, I was two years into my reign as an Olympic swimming champion. I didn't know what I was going to do next with my life, but I knew that I'd reach the summit of an elite international athlete career. Jamie, on the other hand, was a Colonel in the US Army and a Ranger. He knew that his personal ambitions in a military career were being overtaken by the needs of his family. This transition from the military was a voluntary choice he made.

The years since we first met have shown quite a journey for each of us, as we have navigated and curated direction forward as the institutions to which we have spent nearly almost all of our lives no longer provided direction and purpose for us. When Jamie announced that he had written a book about climbing the Manitou Incline, I was excited because I had done the Incline a decade ago while in near-peak athletic shape, having barely entered my 30's. It was a brutal climb even then! So, knowing enough about the goal itself, and knowing a little bit about Jamie the West Point trained army officer I felt it was a reading-journey worth going on. And what I found in that reading was a schema of lessons about life; about goals; about things fixed and about things changeable: a ready guidebook if I needed to re-orient myself to voluntary hardship, along with the wisdom and excellence this produces.

Recently, I visited Jamie in Colorado, and together we did the Incline. Note: Now I am thoroughly out of shape, getting heavier yet weaker each day. I'm no longer the athlete in his prime, nor in the flower of my youth; as fruit has fallen down and inspired the genesis of a little old child of my own. Yes, I'm a father but young to this and still adjusting. Jamie, on the other hand, has got to be at least 10 years my senior, all silver and gray hair cropped close for ease and efficiency; three kids ages twenty-one to fifteen and a wife that has survived a deployment to medical hell and back. Such fortitude; it was not easy for him to wait for me, forcibly going so slow, because I was the one with strength and constitution like a small child.

I tried to pace myself, knowing the journey is hard and steep, alas I depleted early. Nary halfway up the slope I began the self-talk of refusal to give up; an endless stream of this and a thesaurus of similar sentiments--between the pounding of my heart and the labored breathing in the thinning air. Conversation becomes difficult for me so Jamie carries the load a little extra, "It sure is nice to go at this ease of pace. I'm really getting to enjoy the view!" My response is to audibly pant louder. At some point, a pregnant woman jogs up from behind. Jamie recognizes her, and they make some small talk as he waits for me. She jogs by but I'm too tired and focused on one leaden step after another to notice when she disappears from sight up the slope. I can't stop. The mountain will eventually run out of steps, won't it, Sisyphus?

And though the Incline seemed to go on forever steeper, then longer, then steeper again; suddenly Jamie yells, "Almost there! Finish strong!" And he breaks into a sprint up the mountain. I dig deep, recruit all the muscles and neurons—motor and sensory— and sprint after him. And then the end has arrived. I turn around and take in the view.

Anthony Ervin

Anthony Ervin is a four-time Olympic medalist in swimming. In 2016, sixteen years after his first Olympic gold medal, he won the men's 50-meter freestyle for the second time, at the age of 35, becoming the oldest individual Olympic gold medal winner in swimming. He is the author of "Chasing Water: Elegy of an Olympian." He hiked the Incline with the author in April 2023.

AN INTRODUCTION

After a tough 2020 full of COVID restrictions, a friend of mine and I, both in our early 50's, in an effort to challenge ourselves, ward off old age and just as an excuse to spend some time together outdoors, set for ourselves the challenge of climbing up the Manitou Incline in under 30 minutes in 2021 AND climbing the Incline at least once a week all 52 weeks of the year.

For those of you not familiar with the Manitou Incline, it is the converted remains of a funicular railway which goes straight up the side of a mountain and offers great views of Colorado Springs. The first step begins at 6,600 feet above sea level and it gains almost 2,000 feet in just under one mile.

The average grade for the trail is 45% and is as steep as 68% in places. Signs at the bottom of the Incline tell visitors to plan about 2 hours to make the climb. In order to meet our goal of breaking 30 minutes, we agreed to meet every Thursday morning and make the climb. Beginning the first week in January, we would meet at 6 am and trek up the 2700+ steps.

On occasion, one or both of us could not make Thursday morning, so we would make up our session on another day that week—but we always did the hike. We climbed in the dark, in the beating sun, in the rain and wind, hail, snow and every other imaginable type of weather that you would see over the period of a year in Colorado.

During those first cold mornings in January 2021, we averaged about 41 minutes or so from the first step to the last and our goals of 30 minutes seemed foolhardy and certainly out of reach. But as time passed, we slowly, gradually got faster. For me, in situations where I am outside, in nature and exercising intensely, my mind begins to wander. Since we were trying to get faster, I often thought about a) What can I do or what techniques can I employ to shave some seconds off my time? and b) What lessons have I learned or am I learning as a result of putting myself through this punishing physical exercise every week?

After a session on the Incline, I began to write down some of the lessons I was thinking about while hiking. As the lessons began to accumulate, I realized that these were not just lessons for the Incline, but they were lessons for life and for achieving or pursuing any goal. And, like any true-life lesson, I also realized that each maxim that I had "discovered" actually had a Biblical foundation.

How should you read this book? You can certainly sit down and read this straight through in one or two sittings if you want. However, it is designed for you to read it reflectively and introspectively.

I specifically included thirty-one lessons so that no matter what month you choose to begin reading, there will be one lesson per day for the entire month. You can read it over and over each month if you like.

So, let me share with you what I learned, the stories that go with it, questions that you can ask yourself and what the Bible has to say about it. Here we go!

2 HAVE A STRATEGY

Have a strategy for whatever it is that you are trying to accomplish. Both of the verses at the end of this chapter have to do with money, but they can apply to any type of planning. To summarize, if you don't plan well, things could go badly. You would think that climbing the Incline doesn't involve much strategy or planning. You just put one foot in front of the other and climb, right? Well, yes and no. If you actually want to complete the climb, that involves planning, and if you want to do it "fast" that requires a bit of strategy. What am I going to need: Food? Water? What type of clothing? What is the weather forecast? What type of shoes should I wear? What type of socks? Sunblock? Will I need supplemental oxygen? How much time in my schedule do I have to get up, get back down and catch the bus both ways? Do I need a reservation? Do I have a reservation? These and many other considerations should be answered. I cannot tell you how many people I have seen fail on their Incline attempt because they failed to plan. You may not believe it, but I have seen people need to get rescued by paramedics and firefighters from the Incline.

If you are going for speed, there is another whole set of considerations in addition to those above. Now, you are not just concerned about finishing, you are focused on performance. What might you normally bring that will now just slow you down? I used to always wear a Camelback backpack with water, snacks, sunblock, TP and more. When going for speed this year, I carried nothing but my phone and my car key (key, not keys). Then you need to analyze the path. Initially, it is not that steep. Does that mean I start out fast? Are there parts that I can run? Do I go for slow and steady or do I map out places where I can make up time? Do I stop and take breaks or do I push through? I have divided the Incline's 2768 steps into 5-6 pretty recognizable and distinct sections—and I approach these sections differently. Sometimes I climb the same section differently than I did the week before to see if a different technique works better.

A few years ago, during the summer, we had relatives visiting from North Carolina. They wanted to experience the Incline; so, we took them. One member of that party was in decent shape and had at some point in his life run ultra-marathons. His current passion was photography so he brought his high-speed camera along with the equipment bag. He was a classic case of someone without a workable plan. He figured he would just show up and hike to the top. He had difficulties. The altitude, the steepness of the trail, and the heat of the day about wiped him out. I ended up having to go back down the Incline, bring him water, and carry his equipment bag to the top in order for him to finish. It is trite but true, "If you fail to plan, you are planning to fail."

Proverbs 21:15 *The plans of the diligent lead surely to abundance, but everyone who is hasty comes only to poverty.*

Luke 14:28 *Suppose one of you wants to build a tower. Won't you first sit down and estimate the cost to see if you have enough money to complete it?*

Personal Reflections:

What goal(s) are you trying to accomplish?

What is your plan or strategy to accomplish your goals?

How will you ensure that you stick to your strategy?

3 GET ADVICE

Talk to someone who has successfully accomplished what you are trying to achieve. As we began to hit the trail every week, we began to see familiar faces, learn names and become part of the Incline community. There were (and are) people who do the Incline every day. There are people who do the Incline multiple times every day. One guy, set the one-year Incline ascent record by completing it 1,825 times in a 1-year period (I think that record has now been broken). Another guy, affectionately named, Crazy Bob, practically runs up and down the Incline. He once did the Incline 14 times in a 24-hour period.

It is good to talk to these successful and experienced people and get their tips, tricks and hints for what you are trying to accomplish. It makes sense; they have been where I am trying to go. I asked Crazy Bob if he could pace me, but he told me I didn't need a pacer and then offered me several tips. I didn't meet my time goal the next time out, but his advice did help my performance. If someone else has been successful doing the exact same thing that you are trying to do, why not ask them how they've done it and implement what might work for you?

Seeking out and learning from successful individuals, whether through asking for advice or finding a mentor, can be a powerful way to accelerate your progress towards your goals. They can provide valuable insights and advice based on their own experiences, and can help you navigate any challenges or roadblocks that you may encounter along the way.

Finding a mentor can be as simple as reaching out to someone you admire and asking if they would be willing to offer guidance and support. Alternatively, you can join a professional or community organization that offers mentorship programs, or seek out a mentor through a formal mentorship program or platform.

It can also be helpful to simply seek advice from others who have achieved success in your chosen field as I did. This could be through asking for advice directly, or by seeking out resources such as books, articles, or online courses that are written by successful individuals who offer valuable insights and strategies.

Ultimately, seeking out and learning from successful individuals can be a powerful way to boost your own progress towards your goals and can help you navigate your own path to success more effectively and efficiently.

Proverbs 15:22 *Plans fail for lack of counsel, but with many advisers they succeed.*

Me, with Mickey Flowers—probably the nicest person on the Incline.

Personal Reflections:

From whom are you getting advice?

Who can mentor you along your journey?

To whom can you act as a mentor?

4 PREPARE FOR PERFORMANCE

Have you ever noticed what YouTube and Netflix have done by automatically playing the next video or next episode once you have finished the one you selected? They make it easier for you continue watching. They remove all the friction, all the impediments of you starting the next video. When they began this practice, time on their platforms dramatically increased. You can do the same in your personal life. Make it easier to achieve your goals by removing friction, reducing impediments and preparing for performance.

In a previous lesson, I discussed the importance of having a strategy to achieve your goals. While this is a critical step, the best strategy is useless without proper execution of your plan. You have to be intentional not only in executing the strategy but also intentional about setting the conditions for yourself in the actual attempting of your goal(s). Stephen Hawking once said that showing up is half the battle. If you don't even show up, how do you expect to accomplish anything? Being intentional is about showing up. Intentionality is a mindset. You are purposely removing obstacles and excuses that might get in the way of you working on your goals. You must prioritize.

A large component of this lesson, is the realization that I can't solely base my behaviors on how I am feeling. I have to ensure that the performance of the steps to achieve my goal are so much a part of my routine that is almost automatic, which takes how I am feeling out of the equation.

If I based all my actions on how I felt, then I knew that many, many mornings I would not feel like getting up early, going out before dark, often in the cold, and then, punish myself physically. Seriously, who would? Wouldn't it feel better to sleep in, to stay snuggled under the covers with my wife before leisurely getting out of bed and having my coffee? Of course, it would, but if I followed my feelings, I wouldn't accomplish my goals.

So, I did several things to be intentional and remove obstacles that could potentially prevent my getting out every week to do the Incline. I had to make it a priority. How did I do this?

First, I would regularly coordinate with my Incline partner either the day of or the day prior to our hike. This increased my accountability by making sure someone was going to be expecting me that I didn't want to let down.

Next, I would always check the weather the night before to prepare myself mentally for what I was going to encounter. Was it going to be cold, hot, snow, rain, hail, etc.? What would I be facing the next day in my environment besides the 2700+ steps? Checking the weather may seem like a small detail, but it has had a significant impact on my frame of mind and intentionality.

Then, I always made sure that I set my alarm. As mundane and obvious as setting an alarm may seem, it was a critical part of my nightly routine prior to attacking the Incline.

Further, every night before an Incline morning I would set out my clothes. When getting up at 5 a.m. for a 6 a.m. hike, having set out my clothes the night before not only saved me time in the morning but also eliminated at least one decision for early in the morning-what to wear. I didn't have to think about it, I just got dressed. I would start my day with a clear mind and focused on the tasks at hand.

Lastly, I wanted to be intentional about keeping a record of my attempts and my time. Instead of writing down my time in a notebook after tracking it on my watch or phone, I used the sports tracking app, Strava. This app not only kept a record of each time I did the Incline, but also how fast I completed it, and times for different section. It was also a public record for anyone who wanted to see or check in on me.

This idea of intentionality, prioritizing, and showing up applies to so many situations beyond the Incline. This applies to every goal, project or situation in life in which you are trying to achieve something, do something different or get better.

Philippians 3:12 *Not that I have already obtained this or am already perfect, but I press on to make it my own.*

Ephesians 5:15 *Look carefully then how you walk, not as unwise but as wise, making the best use of the time.*

Proverbs 21:5 *The plans of the diligent lead surely to abundance, but everyone who is hasty comes only to poverty.*

<u>Personal Reflection:</u>

In what situations do you need to pay attention to how you are feeling and in what situations should you remove your feelings as a factor in your actions?

In what situations do you need to be more intentional in making sure you show up?

What are some basic steps that you can take to become more intentional and prioritize what is important?

5 GET UP EARLY

For us to be successful in doing the Incline at least one day a week for an entire year, we had to make certain goals a priority. If we waited for a convenient time to pop up every week, something more important would have always come up. If we waited until the end of the day, we likely would feel too tired and offer some lame excuses to each other. We would have failed before we started.

In the chapter "Prepare for Performance" you will recall that as part of my intentionality, I set my alarm every night. I set my alarm because I needed to wake up early. If I wanted to make this goal a priority and if I wanted to make sure I actually did it every week, I would need to do it early before everything else in my busy days crowded out the Incline. It was for this reason that we chose as our time to meet as six o'clock in the morning every Thursday.

Six am sounds early. That's because it is. You may think that getting up that early sounds hard. You're right; it is.

I've been waking up early since even before I started at West Point. You may think, "Well, you're just a morning person." That may be true, but I believe that even "morning people" find it difficult to get out of bed early in the morning. The difference is that they do it. They wake up. They get up. They show up.

Marcus Aurelius, who struggled with, but advocated starting the day early, wrote in what later became the book, "*Meditations,*" "Is this what I was created for? To huddle under the blankets and stay warm?"

I have come to value and protect my morning time. There is something special about the predawn hours before anyone else in the house is stirring, before your family needs you to be present, while most people in your time zone are still sleeping, before stress and the daily tasks of work take hold. The day is fresh, full of energy and pregnant with possibility.

I am most productive and do my best thinking early in the morning. But getting up early is not just about clear thinking and having an undisturbed cup of morning coffee. If there is something that you want to make sure gets done, do it early.

For a year, we met at the parking lot and caught the six am bus up to near the start of the Incline. And guess what? I don't remember a single time where another responsibility interfered at that hour. Our bosses didn't schedule an unexpected meeting at 6 am. Our kids didn't need to be taken to a practice or rehearsal they had forgotten to tell us about. The morning time was always ours.

While we were both sometimes grumpy and really did not feel like being awake or out in the cold and dark, it was always a wonderful feeling of accomplishment when we were done. We had knocked out a priority task for the day or week and we still had the entire day ahead of us. There is something that just makes sense about doing the hardest parts of your day first. By getting hard things out of the way early, they are not hanging over your head all day. You are free to pursue other tasks without worrying about the hardest one still being out there.

Mark 1:35 says *"And rising very early in the morning, while it was still dark, he [Jesus] departed and went out to a desolate place, and there he prayed."*

Jesus Christ exemplified making something a priority and getting up early to do it. Spending time in prayer with God the Father was something He cherished. How did he make sure it happened? He got up early.

How can you accomplish your priorities, the hardest tasks in the day? Get up early.

Psalm 119:147 *I rise early, before the sun is up; I cry out for help and put my hope in your words.*

Genesis 22:3a *So Abraham rose early in the morning, saddled his donkey, and took two of his young men with him, and his son Isaac.*

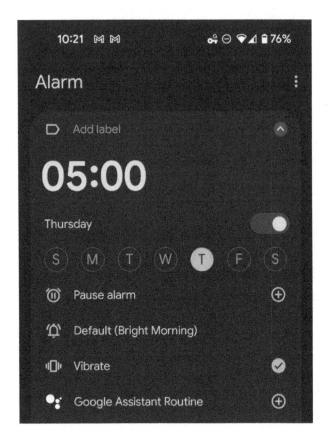

Personal Reflection

What is a daily priority task that you could complete by getting up earlier?

When in the day are you most productive?

How do you protect your productive time?

6 CHOOSE THE RIGHT PATH

There is often more than one way to the top or to achieve your goal-but not all ways are the "right way."

Each of the verses at the end of this chapter describe a road, a path or a way, to get from one place to another. The wisdom implies that there are several directions that one could take on a journey. Depending on your choices, you could encounter "steep and rough" versus "smoothed out," "straight" and the good, restful way. What is the difference between the steep, rough way and the straight, restful way? The difference is who we look to for guidance on the path to take. Are we going to believe God and what He tells us or follow society's philosophy and what it tells us?

There are so many ways to achieve a goal or make it to the top. With the Incline in particular, from the same starting point, I could take a totally different path and end up at the same ending point (see picture at the end of this chapter). The Barr Trail is a windy trail full of switchbacks that has a much more gradual incline, is very beautiful and is about 3-4 miles long. You can follow it up to the top of the Incline. The question I had to ask myself was whether my goal was to get to the top or was my goal to conquer the Incline? When I decided that my goal was to conquer the Incline, then the question I had to ask was "How do I want to do it?" There are so many different strategies and ways to the top as discussed previously—Do I want to bring food and make a fun day of it? Do I rest every 100 steps? Do I take pictures and document my journey? Do I want to take shortcuts or complete the challenge with integrity? I had to choose.

In life we also face obstacles, goals and decisions; and like the Incline, there are many ways to the top and different strategies each way. Some paths look really good, easy and fast—but maybe they are unethical shortcuts. Very tempting. I've been up and down the Barr Trail many times and you can see where many people did not want to follow the path but instead cut through creating or using ugly shortcuts.

Unlike the Incline, we don't have to just ask ourselves what is the correct way, we can look, ask, and lean on the Lord who "smooths out the path." He "makes our path straight" and shows us "the good way."

Isaiah 26:7 *But for those who are righteous, the way is not steep and rough. You are a God who does what is right, and you smooth out the path ahead of them.*

Proverbs 3:5-6 *Trust in the Lord with all your heart and lean not on your own understanding; in all your ways submit to him, and he will make your paths straight.*

Jeremiah 6:16 *Thus says the LORD: Stand by the roads, and look, and ask for the ancient paths, where the good way is; and walk in it, and find rest for your souls.*

Personal Reflections:

How do you want to achieve your goals?

What checks can you set for yourself to ensure you walk the path to goal achievement with integrity?

How can choosing the "wrong way" ultimately prove to be "steep and rough"?

How do you lean on the Lord?

7 PACE YOURSELF

Go at a pace that you can sustain. Starting out too fast can burn you out and exhaust you before you've really even begun. I well remember the beginning days of doing the Incline. At the first step I felt great, mentally and physically. I could do this. Since I felt so good, I decided that I would start out by running. By the 200th step I was smoked—my legs burned, my lungs burned—and I only had 2,568 more steps to go—and I had not even started the steep part yet. I was burned out. The remaining climb was miserable.

I learned pretty quickly to start out at a pace that I could sustain—even if it felt too slow at the beginning. Burnout can result in not finishing what you started.

In the workplace, there are at least 6 factors that contribute to burnout.

1. Unsustainable workload

2. Perceived lack of control of your environment

3. Insufficient rewards for effort

4. Lack of supportive community

5. Lack of perceived fairness

6. Mismatched values and skills

When you are on the Incline you can control many of these factors, some of which are discussed on other pages of this book. When in the workplace, being aware that these situations lead to burnout can go a long way towards prevention.

Just as I Corinthian 9:24 says, in everything we do, we have to approach it in such a way that we are able to give our best performance. Most of life is not a sprint but a marathon.

I Corinthians 9:24: *Do you not know that in a race all the runners run, but only one gets the prize? Run in such a way as to get the prize.*

My daughter, Mia, doing the Incline with me.

Personal Reflections:

What is a situation in which you have experienced burnout?

Do you tend to get excited when starting something new and start out at an unsustainable pace?

What does "pacing yourself" look like for you?

Are any of the six burnout factors relatable to your current situation?

8 STAY FOCUSED

Don't lose focus just because you think you're "finished."

You can't "live" on the mountaintop. Unfortunately, you have to come down from peak experiences. And often, completing your goal is just the beginning of a larger effort.

March 18th, 2021, was a chilly morning—22 degrees with a windchill of 14 degrees. There was a little bit of snow on the ground and the railroad ties steps where definitely frosty. Like most mornings in this condition, we were dressed for the weather and had Yak Trax on our feet. I made it up at a good pace of under 35 minutes. I was feeling pretty good. I had already cut about 5-6 minutes off my January time in just a few short months. I was confident. I was strong. Contrary to what the Incline signs recommend at the bottom of the steps, we headed right back down the steps rather than taking the 4-mile circuitous route down Barr Trail. Walking down the Incline under the very best of conditions is treacherous and not something you can do without full concentration. However, we were confident. We had already done this over 20 times so far this year. This time, about half-way down I put my left foot down on either snow or ice and the Trax did not grip. My feet went out from under me like a cartoon character slipping on a banana peel. No big deal. I had slipped before. This time, as I was coming down, I reached back with my left hand to catch myself—and I did. However, the force of the impact severely dislocated my shoulder and fractured it in two places. So, one second, I am confident, strong, maybe even a bit cocky and the next second, before I even fully realized what had happened, I was about to pass out from the pain. This happens in life too. You've achieved your goal, you are on top of the world and feel like there is nothing that can knock you down.

And then you fall.

It is in often in those moments of success that we need to be most humble and most careful. As financial disclaimers state: "Past performance is no guarantee of future success."

I was half-way down a snow-covered trail, in intense pain, in 20-degree weather and I needed to get to our car and go to an emergency room. This is why we go through life with friends. They are there with you in the good times to celebrate, but they are also there to help you out when you have crashed and burned. I could not have gotten down the mountain without my good arm around my friends' shoulder and his arm around my waist as we both hobbled down.

Note: The technique you see in the movies of slamming your shoulder into a wall or a tree or having someone hit it hard with their hand, does NOT work. We tried it. It hurts!

The two verses below convey exactly what I learned on that snowy trail in March and apply to a wide variety of situations in life.

I Corinthians 10:12 *If you think you are standing strong, be careful not to fall.*

Proverbs 16:18 *Pride goes before destruction, a haughty spirit before a fall.*

Personal Reflections:

How do you make sure you stay humble even when you have a track record of success?

When are you most likely to lose focus and "fall"?

When has your "finish" been just the beginning?

9 BE CONSISTENT

Consistency is a more powerful tool for improvement and goal achievement than motivation.

Motivation can be a powerful driving force in helping you to achieve your goals. It can provide you with the energy, focus, and determination to work towards your objectives. It was motivation that drove me to come up with my two goals (doing the Incline in under 30 minutes and doing the Incline at least once every single week for a year) for this endeavor. But it wasn't necessarily motivation that kept me going day after day.

I found that for me, motivation alone was not enough to guarantee success in achieving these goals. While motivation helped me to get started, it was not sufficient to sustain me over the long term. My motivation often waned. There were many weeks that I was not motivated to get outside in the cold, rain or dark and punish my body at six in the morning.

However, consistency or faithfulness, or steadfastness or perseverance (you choose your word) provided what motivation could not. I found that consistency is particularly important in the pursuit of long-term goals, as it helps to ensure that you stay on track and make steady progress towards your objectives. Developing good habits and routines can help to make your efforts more consistent and sustainable.

I also discovered that consistency helps to build momentum and confidence towards achieving these long-term goals. When we are consistent in our actions towards achieving a goal, we are able to build momentum over time. Apps have discovered this powerful concept with the implementation of streaks. Once you get a good streak going, you don't want to break it and your consistency increases. This was true for me as well. As my streak of consecutive weeks on the Incline increased, my desire to keep the streak going also increased. It was consistency that encouraged me to keep going even when things were tough. In fact, my consistency increased my motivation.

James 1:4 And let steadfastness have its full effect, that you may be perfect and complete, lacking in nothing.

Galatians 6:9 And let us not grow weary of doing good, for in due season we will reap, if we do not give up.

<u>Personal Reflections:</u>

What long-term goal do you want to achieve?

How can you leverage the tool of consistency to help you get there?

How can you use the concept of streaks to help you keep going?

10 FOCUS ON THE NEXT STEP

Depending on the season and situation, your initial steps may be in the dark. That's okay. When whatever you are doing gets hard, just focus on the next step. You can usually, at least, see the next step.

On many occasions, because of daylight savings time, six in the morning is completely dark. You might be able to see the step right in front of you but really not much else. Even when using a headlamp, we could not see very far in front of us. So that forced us to do what we probably should have been doing in the first place—just worrying about the next step—not ALL of the steps in front of us, just the next one.

There is the obvious parallel with living life, completing a project at work, or trying to achieve a personal goal. Ask yourself, "What single step can I take today to get me one step closer to that bigger goal?" or "What small step forward is within reach for me right now?"

If you think about Psalm 119:105 (below), that is essentially what it is saying about the Word of God. It's a lamp. It isn't a sun or a spotlight, but a lamp. A lamp (or headlamp) only lets you see the next few steps on the path. It does not illuminate the entire trail. A lamp doesn't let you see the finish line from the beginning.

When you focus solely on the finish line, the summit, or your ultimate goal, you are unable to focus on what is happening where you are right now. It can be easy to lose sight of the present moment and the small victories that occur along the way. Additionally, looking way ahead can be demoralizing as the distance between where you are and where you want to be can seem insurmountable. If you are already tired and discouraged, looking how much further you have to go may just make you feel like quitting. But if you look down and just think about the next step or two, before you know it, you are at the top. One foot in front of the other; one step at a time.

Ultimately, the key is to find a balance between looking ahead to your ultimate goal and staying present in the journey. By focusing on the next step and making consistent progress, you can move forward in a way that feels both achievable and fulfilling.

Psalm 119:105 *Thy word is a lamp unto my feet and a light unto my path.*

Questions:

What single step can you take today to get you one step closer to your larger goal?

What small step forward is within reach for you?

On what larger goal do you need to stop focusing so much?

11 DON'T COMPARE YOURSELF

Don't worry about what or how everyone else is doing.

I know that I previously wrote that you should talk to other people who have successfully done what you are trying to do, but the flip side of that coin is not to worry about everyone else. Comparison is not only the thief of joy, but comparison, at times, can also hinder your performance when you're trying to achieve your goal.

By nature, we all engage in social comparison. We look at others around us and compare ourselves to them. It can be helpful. For example, if I'm starting the Incline in the middle of a summer afternoon, and I notice that everyone is carrying water and that I am not, then perhaps I should at least look into or ask why they think they need water. Others' performance can also be useful to gauge whether we are "on track."

But comparing ourselves to others can also be harmful. In the case of the Incline, I would look to see how fast or slow others were going and then judge myself based on that. These are subjective comparisons. Obviously, this does not help you get faster.

There were cases when I saw someone faster go by and tried to keep up. For a short time, I would keep up and be a little faster, but in the long run it just made me more tired, discouraged and slower overall.

Other times I went slower than I had the potential to go because I was already passing people—so I thought, "I must be doing pretty well." But again, my performance suffered. I finished slower than I should have.

Over time, I found that it was better to just stick to my plan and strategy and not worry about what everyone else was doing. It was better to establish objective comparisons—times and benchmarks along the path and compare myself to myself and my overall goal.

Matthew 6:27 *And which of you by being anxious can add a single hour to his span of life?*

2 Corinthians 10:12 *We do not dare to classify or compare ourselves with some who commend themselves. When they measure themselves by themselves and compare themselves with themselves, they are not wise.*

<u>Personal Reflections:</u>

How are you measuring yourself and your progress?

Is there someone to whom you should stop comparing yourself?

Are you struggling with imposter syndrome?

What worry do you need to let go of?

12 SEEK CONTINUOUS IMPROVEMENT

You've probably heard the quote, "If you're not getting better you're getting worse." Well, that applies to this lesson.

I knew from my very first day on our Incline challenge that I had a long and difficult road ahead of me. That first day, my time was in the mid-40 minutes. And I was smoked. I was exhausted.

How could I possibly shave fifteen minutes off of my 45-minute time? It seemed like an impossible task.

The reality is that I had to put that discouraging thought out of my head and instead focus on and seek out continuous improvement as a form of encouraging feedback for the time portion of this challenge.

How did I do this?

Despite feeling discouraged by my initial time on the Incline, I knew that I had to focus on continuous improvement to achieve my goal. To accomplish this, I had to change my perspective and approach the challenge in a new way.

First, I had to realize that continuous improvement did NOT mean that I would get faster each time that I climbed the Incline. It just wasn't going to happen. But I did want my general trend over time to show improvement. Have you ever been on a diet and wanted to lose ten or so pounds? Your weight will fluctuate. You may be down six pounds and then find a couple days later that it is only four and then the next week it is eight. You are trending in the right direction.

Also, I didn't want to just go by how I felt or what I remembered. So, I made sure to have a method to track over time. For me, I used the fitness app, Strava, which would keep my overall times, my times on different parts of the Incline and show me my trends over time.

This attitude and perspective helped me stay motivated and keep my momentum when progress felt slow or when it seemed I wasn't improving quickly enough.

It was also this mindset of constant improvement that led to me discover many of the lessons contained in this book. Every time that I would hike, I would try to identify and address potential issues or obstacles that were slowing me down and make the necessary adjustment either on the fly or the next time out.

However, seeking continuous improvement wasn't just about tracking my progress and making adjustments. It also required me to stay open to new tips, tactics, and techniques that could help me achieve my goal. By staying adaptable and flexible, I was able to incorporate new approaches that worked and let go of those that didn't.

Lastly, the mentality of seeking continuous improvement allowed me to stay adaptable and flexible in my approach to my goal. If someone offered me a new tip, tactic or technique, I would try it out. I didn't feel the pressure to achieve my best time every time out. If the advice worked, I would incorporate it; if it didn't I would let it go.

In my pursuit of continuous improvement on the Incline, I learned valuable lessons that can be applied to any aspect of life. By staying focused on the goal, tracking progress, staying adaptable, and open to new ideas, we can achieve improvement in any area we choose

This lesson reminds me of the Frederick Nietzsche quote.

> The essential thing 'in heaven and
> earth' is that there should be a long
> obedience in the same direction;
> there thereby results, and has always
> resulted in the long run, something
> which has made life worth living.

The phrase "long obedience in the same direction; there thereby results" speaks to me of making continuous progress over time resulting in improvement.

Galatians 6:9 *And let us not grow weary of doing good, for in do season we will reap, if we do not give up.*

Hebrews 11:1 *Now faith is the assurance of things hoped for, the conviction of things not yet seen.*

Hebrews 6:11 *We want each of you to show this same diligence to the very end, so that what you hope for may be fully realized.*

Personal Reflection:

What area of your life would you to like see consistent improvement?

What mechanisms or tools can you use to help you see that progress over time?

How will you identify and document either impediments to success and/or techniques for improvement?

13 GO WITH A FRIEND

Striving for your goal with at least one other person provides accountability, camaraderie and enjoyment along the journey. This entire venture started when I mentioned to my friend what I was thinking about doing. He volunteered, "If you do it, I will do it with you!"

There are many advantages to pursuing a challenge with a friend. First, another person striving with you provides accountability—both ways—for you and them. I cannot tell you how many dark, cold, early mornings when my alarm went off at 5 am, that I just wanted to hunker down under the covers and go back to sleep. But knowing my buddy was going be there to meet me and was counting on me to be there, forced me to get up, get dressed, make the drive, take the bus and do the Incline. I was always glad afterwards that I showed up, but I knew that I probably would not have if John had not been there to meet me.

Second, having someone on your goal journey with you provides and/or strengthens friendship and camaraderie. I'm sure that you are aware that loneliness in our society has reached epidemic proportions. It is often even worse for middle-age or older men. It has been said that suffering from loneliness has the same detrimental health effects of smoking 15 cigarettes per day. Find someone to achieve a goal with or to do a regular activity with. Just ask them. Chances are, they will jump at the chance.

Similarly, just like in most activities in life, the experience of doing the Incline was much more enjoyable and fun when doing it with a friend. We would catch up on each other's lives during the bus ride up, talk about life and how we were feeling, discuss our Incline strategy for that day and often just chat during the first part of the hike. We did the same thing in reverse after summitting. Eventually, if time permitted we would often grab a coffee after the Incline and continue to build a friendship. It was fun!

I will talk about it more later, but having a friend with you in a time of need is essential.

Lastly, just as Proverbs 27:17 says, we sharpened one another. Having a buddy made both of us better. I know the fact of accountability, camaraderie and enjoyment actually helped each of us, over time, hike the Incline better and faster.

Proverbs 27:17: *As iron sharpens iron, so one person sharpens another.*

Proverbs 17:17 *A friend loveth at all time, And a brother is born for adversity.*

The boys in the picture are my son, Noah (L), and his neighbor buddy, Jonas (R), at the top of the Incline with me.

Personal Reflections:

Do you have a friend who will encourage you and hold you accountable as you go through life or try to achieve "hard things?"

Who can you ask to join you on your challenge or venture towards goal completion?

Who is striving to achieve a goal right now or going through some adversity where you could join in?

14 ENJOY THE JOURNEY

Take time to enjoy the journey—look around you, experience beauty—sights and sounds.

It is very tempting when doing the Incline or really when trying to accomplish any goal to just put your head down, focus on achievement and tune everything else out. That is usually what I did (and do).

But every once in a while, while climbing, I would stop to look around or take a picture; the beauty is overwhelming. You may be familiar with the Ralph Waldo Emerson quote: "It is not the destination. It is the journey." That is very true in accomplishing other goals or completing projects as well. Often times, when you are trying to do hard things, the reward is in the trying!

This definitely became true for me on the Incline. While I still strove all year to break the 30-minute barrier, the journey towards that goal really became what was important to me rather than the "destination" of breaking 30 minutes.

On a side note, I did do one Incline hike when all that I did was try to look and listen to everything around me—the beauty and all the different sounds—only paying attention to that. I really tuned out everything else—how much further I had to go, what my time was, how tired I was feeling. In my mind, that trip passed very quickly and by the clock, it was one of my faster ascents of the year. It's important to remember that the journey towards any goal is just as important as the goal itself.

Psalm 96:11-12 *Let heaven celebrate! Let the earth rejoice! Let the sea and everything in it roar! Let the countryside and everything in it celebrate! Then all the trees of the forest too will shout out joyfully.*

Job 12:7-10 *But ask the beasts, and they will teach you; the birds of the heavens, and they will tell you; or the bushes of the earth, and they will teach you; and the fish of the sea will declare to you. Who among all these does not know that the hand of the Lord has done this? In his hand is the life of every living thing and the breath of all mankind.*

My wife, Allison, doing the Incline with me.

Personal Reflections:

When was the last time you took a break or really paid attention to what was going on around you?

Are you fully present when you need to be?

What is it like for you to cultivate silence, slow down and think   deeply?

15 KEEP MOVING FORWARD

Don't stay too long on a single step or section, keep moving!

Like completing the Incline, accomplishing a goal or finishing a project is usually a series of steps forward.

Don't get stuck or stay too long on a single step. Keep moving forward.

It is fine to stop, look around, re-group and enjoy the beauty of the trip, but you don't want to get stuck on a step. In a project, getting stuck on a step may mean trying to get it perfect or maybe feeling like you just don't have the energy to continue.

Perfection can be the enemy of the good. In contrast, focusing on being "good enough" allows us to make progress and achieve our goals without getting bogged down by the pursuit of perfection. It allows us to be more flexible and adaptable, and to learn and grow as we go. By accepting that we are not perfect and that it is okay to make mistakes, we can move forward with confidence and resilience (more on this later).

Of course, this doesn't mean that we shouldn't strive for excellence or put quality effort into our work. It simply means that we should be mindful of the balance between perfection and progress, and recognize that sometimes good, is good enough. By letting go of the need for perfection, we can achieve our goals and make meaningful progress in a more sustainable and enjoyable way.

On the Incline, without running, you really don't want to leave your foot on the step for any longer than you need too. It actually takes more energy to take "heavy" steps-pausing on each step. When you stop or pause, you not only lose momentum but lactic acid and fatigue set into your legs. You get slower. As a general rule, it is best to keep moving forward at a good steady pace.

Just as it takes more energy to take "heavy" steps on the Incline, getting stuck on a step in a project can also drain energy and motivation. When we stop and linger on one step, we lose momentum and can become fatigued. Keep moving forward!

Progress not perfection!

Job 17:9a *The righteous keep moving forward*

Personal Reflections:

Do you let "the perfect" become the enemy of "the good?"

What do you need to let go of in order to keep you moving forward?

How do you maintain your momentum?

16 BEWARE OF FALSE SUMMITS

Beware of false summits. They can be demoralizing.

A false peak or false summit is a peak that appears to be the pinnacle of the mountain but upon reaching it, it turns out the summit is higher and further away.

If you are continuously focused too far ahead, you may think you are close to reaching your goal when in fact it is a false summit. You may think that you have almost arrived when in reality, you still have a long way to go.

We have all seen in sports, the football player who is celebrating on his way to the end zone and someone catches him, tackles him or knocks the ball out of his hands. Or the team that thinks they have won, only for the other team to come back and deliver a knockout punch in the final seconds of the game.

This can happen to us too. If you look closely at the next picture of the Incline or if you are doing it in person—the top that you see there is NOT the top. But if you don't know that, you set your goal for the wrong point. You mentally and emotionally condition yourself to think, "When I reach that point, I am done." And then when it proves to be false, it can be crushing.

This happened to me (and many people) the first time I attempted the Incline. It also happens in life. I focus on a single point thinking it is the finish line only to discover, that I am only partially complete. Or I start celebrating as I get close to what I think is the end only to discover that I surged too soon and maybe don't have enough energy to finish well. If you're competing against someone or another team, perhaps the letdown causes you to get passed by or beaten by your competitors.

What can you do? Be aware. Have humility. Be mentally tough.

I believe that this is the message of Proverbs 11:2. Think about the sports examples that I gave previously—their pride came before their disgrace, but with humility comes wisdom (and success).

Proverbs 11:2 *When pride comes, then comes disgrace, but with humility comes wisdom.*

Personal Reflections:

Have you ever had an experience where you let down before crossing the finish line or completing a goal?

What could potentially be a "false summit" in a project that you are currently working on or a goal that you have set for yourself?

17 FIND INSPIRATION

What is the point or purpose behind what you are trying to accomplish or achieve? Many know Simon Sinek for his books and talks about discovering your "why" or finding your purpose. When faced with a challenging goal or task, it can be easy to feel overwhelmed or discouraged. It is in these moments that finding inspiration and purpose can be crucial to staying motivated and pushing through obstacles. Without a strong sense of purpose and inspiration, the road to achieving a difficult goal can feel daunting and even impossible.

In a previous chapter of this book I discussed how and why I found that consistency was more powerful and more important than motivation. This is especially true for long-term tasks, goals and projects. For me, without a doubt consistency is more important over time. However, even within these enduring goals, which in my case was a year-long goal, there were individual days where consistency got me to the base on the Incline, it got me to show up, but it took motivation to get me to the top.

There were many days that I wanted to quit a quarter of the way up, half-way or even three-fourths of the way up the Incline. I wanted to turn around and go back home. I didn't because I relied on inspiration and motivation. I had to tap into intrinsic motivation, which is often more powerful than external motivators like rewards or recognition (plus, there were no external motivators).

My inspiration and how I practiced it was really a form of self-talk which I discussed previously. When I did not feel motivated but needed motivation, I would usually think about and picture one of three people in my head. I found that visualizing certain people and their remarkable achievements helped me stay motivated during the toughest moments of my Incline challenge.

The first person who I would often think about was Tyler. Tyler was a Paralympic sit-skier silver medalist that I met several years ago. In general, he is a pretty awesome guy, and just what he achieves on a daily basis is inspirational. However, after I met him, I discovered that in 2013 he scaled the Manitou Incline ON HIS HANDS! So, when I am feeling down and out and sorry for myself and wanting to quit, I think about Tyler.

Next, is Rachel. Rachel is a friend I made while on the Incline. For a period of time, she held the record for most ascents in a year by female (over one thousand). I would see her almost every time I went because she was always there. There were many days where she did twelve Incline summits within a 24-hour period. That was inspiring, but where she really tipped the scales for me was when she became pregnant and continued (with her doctor's blessing) to do the Incline. She ended up doing over 500 Incline summits while pregnant. You can see in the photograph that she is holding up eight fingers; showing that she is eight months pregnant. Her baby has done the Incline more times than I have. If she can continue to do the Incline while pregnant, what do I have to complain about? Inspiring!

Last, but certainly not least, my inspiration is my wife, Allison. She has done the Incline several times, although it really isn't her thing. She inspires me because of her fierce resilience and positive attitude in the face of adversity. In defiance of a terminal cancer diagnosis, she did not wilt and give up but instead pushed harder. While enduring nearly twenty surgeries over her lifetime, she educated herself, changed her life and has assisted countless others since the diagnosis in 2015. If she can endure the continuous, momentous fact of cancer, then I can certainly endure through a temporary discomfort of my ultimately trivial Incline challenge.

As I thought about these three people while climbing, they helped me stay focused and motivated but more importantly their examples helped me maintain proper perspective. They served as my inspiration.

Psalm 57:2 *I cry out to God Most High, to God who fulfills his purpose for me.*

Proverbs 20:5 *The purposes of a person's heart are deep waters, but one who has insight draws them out.*

Hebrews 12:1 *therefore, since we are surrounded by such a great cloud of witnesses, let us throw off everything that hinders and the sin that so easily entangles. And let us run with perseverance the race marked out for us.*

Me, with Rachel Jones—still going strong at eight months pregnant.

Personal Reflection:

Do you know your why, your purpose, behind what you are trying to achieve?

Who or what for you serves as inspiration when you require a little extra motivation?

What is it about that person that serves as motivation for you?

18 SET INTERMEDIATE GOALS

Set intermediate goals. Celebrate along the way—and at the end.

In my head, I have broken the Incline up into different phases or benchmarks along the way. They let me know how I am doing. Those are my objective measures. For example, I may say that I want to reach step 1600 within 15 minutes. Or maybe, I'll take a short rest at step 1000. These intermediate goals also gave me the opportunity to pause, look back and see how far I had already come. Seeing progress for me was always an encouragement to continue upwards. Also, since the steps are numbered (there is a metal marker ever 100th step), it is easy to celebrate each of these milestones.

While my speed goal was to do the Incline in under 30 minutes, I knew I would not achieve that right away. So, for example, if my very first time was 43 minutes, then I would set a goal for 40 minutes and celebrate when I achieved that milestone, then 38 minutes, 35 minutes and so on. If I didn't make it every time, I wouldn't beat myself up. I would remind myself of the truism, that is especially true on a cold, dark morning on the Incline, that "half the battle is just showing up."

It was not unusual to be consistently finishing the Incline in the mid-30 minutes and then out of nowhere have a slower, 40+ minute climb. Did that setback cause me to stop doing it or quit? No. It is similar to any goal in any environment, whether that is finishing an educational degree, finding a new job, finalizing a project or even losing weight. You celebrate your mini-achievements while not letting setbacks demoralize you. Setbacks will happen. You will gain weight when you are trying to lose it. You won't get hired for every job to which you apply. You might fail an assignment on the way to your degree. As I previously mentioned, this is where having a friend or a partner along on the journey with you has benefits. You celebrate one another's achievements and pick one another up when you fall.

On the Incline, everyone celebrates and congratulates one another when they reach the top—it doesn't matter if you did it in 20 minutes or two and a half hours. It doesn't matter if you are with friends or it is someone you have never laid eyes on before. You celebrate the finish! I wonder in what other areas of life we can practice this?

2 Timothy 4:7-8 *I have fought the good fight, I have finished the race, I have kept the faith. Now there is in store for me the crown of righteousness, which the Lord, the righteous Judge, will award to me on that day.*

Matthew 25:21 *Well done thy good and faithful servant.*

<u>Personal Reflections:</u>

What is an intermediate goal that you can set for yourself now to work towards?

What ways do or can you celebrate goal accomplishment?

19 BE OPEN TO OPPORTUNITY

I had my fastest time on the Incline on a day that I wasn't even supposed to be there. I hadn't planned to go that day because my hiking buddy and I had already done our one Incline previously that week.

It was a hot August day; I got off work a little early and was feeling antsy. So, I said to myself, "I'm going to burn off this energy on the Incline." And, off I went.

It was a great day. I felt great. I felt strong and my energy stayed at a high level the entire time. It was my fastest time to date. I would not have even been there if I had not been flexible and open to spontaneity.

I've found that the benefits of a mindset of openness didn't end there – in fact, it extended to people that I met on the Incline. I found it to be important to not be so focused on my goals that I would not allow myself to be interrupted. If I had not permitted myself to be "interruptible," I would have never met all the great friends on the Incline.

One of the great aspects of doing this challenge was meeting regulars on the Incline, stopping, talking or comparing notes and getting to know them. If I had been only goal-focused, I would have missed out on one of the best aspects of doing the Incline regularly. Being open to other possibilities was key to meeting these new friends and having an even more enriching experience on the Incline.

Have you ever noticed how often in Biblical account that Jesus got interrupted? He seemed to welcome these seeming distractions. Many of the miracles that Jesus performed and that were recorded in the Gospels happened during what seemed like an interruption or a disruption in what Jesus had been currently doing or had planned for the day. Think of all the people that Jesus healed after he had been interrupted from what he was originally doing. Imagine how different the narrative would have been if Jesus were annoyed with these unplanned events and not open to changes in his schedule. You can really take any of the stories, but I envision the story that I used to hear in Sunday School where Jesus was teaching inside a house that was so crowded with people that no one could get in or out. So, a crippled man's friends carried him to the top of the house, ripped a hole in the roof and lowered their friend down to be healed. If I were Jesus, I would have probably looked up and said something like, "Hey, can't you see I'm speaking here? I'm about to get to my main point. Why don't you make an appointment on my Outlook calendar and I'll see if maybe I can help you then?"

So, what can we learn from Jesus's example? If you pay attention you will notice a pattern. Jesus allowed himself to be interrupted by others, and when he did, "good things" happened. Maybe it's not just about being open to interruptions or disruptions, but actively seeking out opportunities in them.

What if, like Jesus, you look for opportunities instead of the annoyances in the interruptions of life? What if you allow yourself to be interrupted for the express purpose of seeing what "good things" can come out of those situations?

You might not heal anyone, but you might help someone and I can almost guarantee that it will help change your attitude.

Be spontaneous. Be interruptible. Be flexible. By having a mindset of openness, we can avail ourselves to new experiences and opportunities for personal growth and achievement.

Proverbs 19:21 *Many are the plans in a person's heart, but it is the Lord's purpose that prevails.*

James 4: 13-14 *Now listen, you who say, 'Today or tomorrow we will go to this or that city, spend a year there, carry on business and make money.' Why, you do not even know what will happen tomorrow. What is your life? You are a mist that appears for a little while and then vanishes. Instead, you ought to say, 'If it is the Lord's will, we will live and do this or that.'*

<u>Personal Reflection</u>:

Think of an instance where an interruption led to a good outcome.

Where in your life do you need to allow or make room for more spontaneity?

Do you have a mindset and attitude of interruptibility?

20 GIVE ENCOURAGEMENT

Encouraging someone else literally costs you nothing, but it can mean everything.

Have you ever worked really hard at something but no one seemed to notice or give you any recognition or feedback? Or have ever been struggling with a project or goal and just needed a bit of encouragement to let you know that you were on the right track? Have you ever felt like you wanted to quit, but just at the right moment someone came along and motivated you to keep going?

Encouragement is something we all need to keep us motivated or to give us confidence that we are at least doing "okay." And, like most altruistic behavior, there is as much benefit in giving encouragement as in receiving it.

Even the most positive, motivated person can experience discouragement on the Incline.

Incliners like to say, "You may get faster, but the Incline never gets easier." Anyone out on the Incline, no matter how slow or out of shape they may be or even if they are a superstar, deserves encouragement because they are out there trying to do something hard.

The Incline becomes a "micro community" for everyone who is on it and attempting it at a particular moment-- because you are all in it together. People say "Good morning!" or "Nice job!" or "You're almost there!" or "You're doing great!" or "Are you okay?" Or, as a young soldier said to me as I was coming down and he was going up with his unit, "Sir, I want to be like you when I'm OLD." I am NOT old, but I knew what he meant. It was encouraging.

Getting encouragement keeps you going when you want to quit and speeds you up when you want to slow down. Plus, giving encouragement is often as life-giving as receiving it.

What if we applied this principle of encouragement that our Incline "micro community" practices to everyday life? What if we took a moment to say "Hello," or "Nice job!" or "You're doing great!" or "Are you okay?" when we encounter others in the other "micro communities" in which we travel every day?

I Thessalonians 5:12 *Therefore encourage one another and build one another up, just as you are in fact doing.*

Romans 15:12 *Each of us should please our neighbors for good, to build them up.*

<u>Personal Reflections:</u>

Who can you encourage today?

How can you ensure that you get the encouragement and feedback that you require?

21 TAKE A BREAK

Realize that sometimes you may need to pause, catch your breath, rest and/or regroup before moving on.

Have you ever been working on a goal or project and you are so tired or unfocused that you finally realize that to continue working would actually be counterproductive? In this state you are likely to make errors that you will have to go back later and fix. I'm sure that we can all relate to reading a page of a book or an instruction manual; you get to the end and have no idea what you just read. It is time to take a break!

We were made to take a rest. God modeled this for us when he rested on the seventh day of creation and there are many instances of Jesus resting. My favorite is when he was sleeping on the boat in the middle of a storm. Some days you need to take a rest in the middle of a storm.

Depending on what you are doing, if you are not performing at your optimal level you could injure yourself. Perhaps you are under the weather, already injured or just plain tired. Rest!

I have had many days on the Incline just like this. I remember one day in September, after I had been doing the Incline weekly for nine months and had a best time of 31 minutes, I tackled the Incline like I always did. But I could just feel in my bones that I was tired. Something felt off. On three separate occasions, I felt dizzy and was in danger of falling backwards down or off the stairs. It was dangerous. I realized that I just neede to pause, rest and regroup before continuing up. I ended up having to stop several times—even sitting down. My time that day was about 43 minutes—slower than my first hike of the year. While disappointed, I knew if I had not rested I could have seriously injured myself in my quest.

In a long or arduous project, sometimes we just need to rest and regroup and come back stronger on another day. Continuing on when we should take a break is actually more detrimental in the long run.

Hebrews 4:10 *For anyone who enters God's rest also rests from their works, just as God did from his.*

Genesis 2:3 *And God blessed the seventh day and declared it holy, because it was the day when He rested from all His work of creation.*

Psalm 91:1 *Whoever dwells in the shelter of the Most High will rest in the shadow of the Almighty.*

Personal Reflections:

What does rest look like for you?

What are the warning signs or triggers that let you know it is time to take a break and regroup?

22 EXPECT THE UNEXPECTED

The best laid plans . . .. While it is useful to have a plan and a strategy, something will surprise you. You can believe that you have thought of everything, but accidents, misfortune or unexpected events can still strike. In our area of Colorado, one of the biggest x-factors is the weather. You can try to plan for the weather, but more often than not the forecast is wrong. We have done the Incline in snow, rain, sleet, fog, wind, lightning and every other conceivable type of weather—usually not forecast. Another unplanned event is an injury-a slip or fall. If you are a regular on the Incline, it is not a question of if you are going to fall and get injured, but when and how severe the injury will be. More about that later.

Finally, the condition of the Incline varies as well. With so much traffic (it has become a tourist attraction), the trail changes—usually for the worse. Steps get dislodged or disappear and gaping holes appear where they once were not. You can't predict it. You can't plan for it. And you can't control it. As Ecclesiastes says, "chance happen to them all."

In real life, outside of the "Incline bubble," Proverbs 16:9 (below) is both more sobering and more comforting. To paraphrase, we think we are in control and we plan what we are going to do, but ultimately the Lord is in control, and he will reveal your next steps.

In 2015, our family had the next 3-5 years of our life planned. Life was good, and we knew what we were doing. I was a Colonel in the Army, and the Army was sending me to London for a year with my family to attend a British version of our War College. My children were going to go to a private school for children of diplomats (paid for by the government), and following that year we would receive another three-year assignment in Europe—one of our favorite places. But then the unexpected happened. Unplanned snow, rain and lightning came pouring down. We found out that my wife, Allison, had a severe, metastatic breast cancer. While we had planned our course, the Lord had a different path he wanted our family to travel. As Mike Tyson once quipped, "Everyone has a plan until they get punched in the mouth."

Ecclesiastes 9:11 *I have seen something else under the sun: The race is not to the swift or the battle to the strong, nor does food come to the wise or wealth to the brilliant or favor to the learned; but time and chance happen to them all.*

Proverbs 16:9 *In their hearts humans plan their course, but the Lord establishes their steps.*

Personal Reflections:

How do you plan for the unforeseen?

Is your strategy flexible enough to respond to the unexpected?

Whom are you trusting for your future?

23 TALK TO YOURSELF

Just like in life, or in pursuing a goal or working to accomplish tasks in a project, I found that there are days on the Incline that are just harder than other days.

Perhaps I didn't sleep well, maybe I was sore from a workout the day before, possibly there were poor weather conditions or some other factor that just made that day more difficult.

I have previously discussed several mechanisms or techniques to power through those types of days: such as "Go with a Friend" or "Give (and receive) Encouragement." Believe me, I personally practice all of my Lessons from the Incline, especially when I am struggling.

However, one day (there have been more than one), I found myself on the Incline really struggling and I wanted to quit. I was hiking alone; there were very few other Incliners hiking that day. I wanted to turn around where I was and just go back down.

Nobody would ever know.

But I would know.

Consistency brought me to the foot of the Incline, but it would take a bit of motivation to get me to the top.

That's when I started talking to myself.

I have a background in psychology, so I know the power of self-talk, and I realize that we always have an internal dialogue going on in our head (if you just said, "No I don't" that's it). But that day I started deliberately talking to myself.

I would like to say that I followed the psychological principles of positive self-talk and only said encouraging words and sentences such as:

"I am strong and capable of doing this." Or "I am focused and determined to succeed."

I remember telling myself, "This is what I love about the Incline—the struggle." And "Come on, Jamie, you can do this."

But suddenly, my inner voice kicked into drill sergeant mode and started yelling at me, calling me names and accusing me of being a lazy quitter. I realize that for some, this is an example of negative self-talk and exactly the type of inner dialogue that is harmful, the type of self-talk that you want to avoid. But for me, with my military background, that voice was pretty motivating. I didn't turn around. I didn't quit. I self-talked myself to the summit.

There are many well-documented benefits of positive self-talk. I found these three to be particular useful for me:

1. It boosts motivation. Self-talk can help boost motivation and keep you focused on the task at hand. By using positive self-talk, you can encourage yourself to push through difficult moments and stay committed to completing the challenge.

2. It enhances confidence. Positive self-talk can also enhance your confidence and belief in your abilities. By reminding yourself of your past successes and strengths, you can build a sense of self-assurance that will help you tackle the challenge with greater ease.

3. It controls anxiety. Self-talk can also be used to control anxiety or nervousness before and during the challenge. By using calming self-talk phrases, you can help alleviate any stress or anxiety you may be feeling, which can improve your performance.

Self-talk, of course, can take other forms. It can be a note to yourself on your mirror or refrigerator. It can be something that you say over and over to yourself in order to achieve a desired outcome. Or it could be a quote that motivates you. Do whatever works for you.

Philippians 4:8 *Finally, brothers and sisters, whatever is true, whatever is noble, whatever is right, whatever is pure, whatever is lovely, whatever is admirable—if anything is excellent or praiseworthy—think about such things*

Proverbs 23:7a *For as a man thinks in his heart so is he.*

Personal Reflection:

What does self-talk look like for you?

When do you deliberately engage in self-talk?

Is your self-talk encouraging, instructive or berating?

24 ADAPT AND OVERCOME

The path is different throughout the trail—some steep, some not quite as steep. You can't have the same approach or technique for different parts of the trail or you will stumble, fall and fail. You must adapt to changing situations and circumstances in order to overcome unexpected obstacles.

One of the great features of the Incline is the varied terrain. There is nothing uniform about the steps or the path. While the warning sign at the bottom compares the Incline to climbing structures such as the Empire State Building or the Statue of Liberty, there is really no comparison. The steps in those two structures are uniform and standard throughout. You can step up each step the same way. Your approach is the same. Not so on the Incline.

There are sections where the steps are maybe two inches tall and others where each step is about 36 inches tall. There are places where you can take the steps two at a time and places where both feet have to hit the step before taking the next one. Some steps have boulders as part of them and some steps have holes in them. As a result, you have to approach each section differently. There is a quote attributed to Albert Einstein where he said that the definition of insanity is "doing the same thing over and over again and expecting different results." On the Incline, I would change that and say that the definition of insanity is doing the same thing over and over again and expecting the SAME results. If the terrain or the situation (or step) has changed, you must adapt your approach accordingly.

This principle applies to just about any goal that has different steps or where the situation can change. Even if you are following a very defined algorithm with ten distinct steps, it is likely that if you try to follow the same method to solve each step that you will fail. Assess the next step in your process, determine what will work best, and then do it.

The verses below speak to how in different situations or circumstances, one might need to take a different approach.

Mark 9:28-29 *Afterward, when Jesus was alone in the house with his disciples, they asked him, "Why couldn't we cast out that evil spirit?" Jesus replied, "This kind can be cast out only by prayer."*

1 Corinthians 9:19 *For though I am free from all, I have made myself a servant to all, that I might win more of them.*

Hebrews 7:12 *For when the priesthood is changed, the law must be changed also.*

Personal Reflections:

Have you ever followed a step in a process even when it didn't seem to apply?

How do you incorporate flexibility into your goal achievement?

25 GET OUTSIDE

Walking/hiking outside focuses your thoughts and reduces stress.

There were many times over the course of the year where I felt unmotivated, tired, stressed and even depressed. And I did not want to do the Incline. But I showed up because I knew I was meeting someone (see Chapter, "Go with a Friend"). However, there was not one single time, regardless of how I felt before I began, that I did not feel better at the end and was glad that I completed it. I remember one morning in particular. I met my buddy for the 6 am bus as normal. He looked like he had not slept a wink, and he confirmed my suspicion. He had not. He told me that a project he was getting ready to begin and had already put a lot of time, work and money into was now in doubt if it would even happen. He didn't know what to do. He couldn't sleep. He was anxious and the stress was almost overwhelming. In fact, he told me that he probably wouldn't even finish the Incline that morning. He said for me to just go up without him and that he would rejoin me on the way down. He was just too exhausted.

Well, he **did** finish that morning, and he had one of his better times. By the time we made it down, he was less stressed, in a better mood and his perspective had changed. He emailed me the next day and wrote: "I think the Incline woke me up and got me productive yesterday. It was good to hit the trail again."

Psalm 23:2, 3a says: *He lets me rest in green meadows; he leads me beside peaceful streams. He renews my strength.*

Isn't this portion of Psalm 23 a beautiful picture? You can just picture the serenity of the scene. I believe there is something about being outside, in the green meadows, beside peaceful streams that literally reduces stress and renews your strength. The scene in the next picture is along the Barr Trail, an alternate, safer way down to the bottom of the Incline—other than going back down the steps. And during wildflower season in Colorado I occasionally like to come down this way just to bathe in the beauty of Colorado. There is something about the mountain air, the beauty and just being outside that is so refreshing! The Japanese have a word for this, *shinrin-yoku*, which translates to forest bathing. A large body of research has shown that being outdoors in the woods, reduces stress, improves immunity, decreases depression, focuses your thoughts, increases creativity and even helps you sleep better. For me, I have my best thoughts while walking outside in the woods. Every lesson that I have written about in this book, I formed while climbing up the steps in the woods.

Nietzsche wrote, "The only ideas won by walking have any value."

<u>Personal Reflections:</u>

Do you make time to get outside, unplug and enjoy the benefits that nature has to offer?

If you cannot be outside in the woods, what else might be a workable alternative?

Where do you do your deepest, most productive thinking?

26 SURROUND YOURSELF WITH EXCELLENCE

Speaker Jim Rohr is purported to have originated the saying that you are the average of the five people you spend the most time with. A similar corollary quote is, "Show me your friends and I will show you your future."

I wanted my future on the Incline to be one of speed and consistency, so those are the people that I sought out and surrounded myself with. My small, personal Incline Challenge was nothing compared to the performances of some of the people that I met, became friends with, and with whom I interacted weekly. There were many people who did the Incline every single day. I became friends with Incliners who were members of the 500 Club (500 or more ascents in a 365-day period). There were several athletes who summitted the Incline much, much faster than I could or would ever do. Then there were those so dedicated that they climbed the Incline multiple times every day.

The people who you spend the most time with in a particular aspect of life will shape who you are in that part of your life. I've heard that if you spend all your time with five millionaires, you will be the sixth. Your crowd, or tribe, can affect what attitudes that you hold and what behaviors you exhibit. You will start to think and behave like those with whom you are spending the most time. While this principle works in the positive direction, it goes the other way too. If you spend all your time with five criminals, you will be the next one spending time in jail.

This principle of surrounding yourself with excellence became particularly clear to me when I intentionally became part of a group of people dedicated to excellence on the Incline, including my Incline buddy, John. Although in a previous lesson I cautioned against comparing yourself to others, surrounding yourself with excellence just naturally raises the bar and establishes a culture of higher standards that you become part of.

The most important person in my "group of five" was my weekly hiking co-challenger, John. I wrote previously in the "Go with a Friend" lesson about many of the advantages of embarking on a challenge, adventure, or goal accomplishments with a friend. One advantage that I failed to mention, was that the friends can provide each other healthy competition, and this competition can improve your performance.

The Williams sisters, Venus and Serena, were very close personally, but they were also very competitive and as a result they made each other better tennis players. John and I have a similar dynamic. We never raced. We both climbed at our own speed. Sometimes, he was faster than I was, and sometimes, I was faster than he. And although we weren't trying to beat one another to the top, I would be lying if I said that I didn't want to be first every time. As a result, we established a culture of excellence and that helped each other get better and faster.

Remember, it is important to carefully choose who we spend our time with because our relationships can have a significant impact on our personal growth and success or failure. When we surround ourselves with individuals who are dedicated and determined, we are more likely to work toward achieving our own goals. Additionally, we are likely to be inspired and motivated by their example of success, and our own goals appear more attainable.

This principle does not just apply to goal achievement. Do you want to be more generous? Do you want to be more kind? Do you want to be more thoughtful? Do you want to be healthier? Do you want to become more spiritual? Find the people that do it well and begin spending time with them. It will change your life.

I Corinthians 15:33 *Do not be misled: 'Bad company corrupts good character.'*

Proverbs 22:24-25 *Do not make friends with a hot-tempered person, do not associate with one easily angered, or you may learn their ways and get yourself ensnared.*

Proverbs 27:17 *As iron sharpens iron, so one person sharpens another.*

Hebrews 10:24 *And let us consider one another to provoke unto love and to good works.*

<u>Personal Reflection:</u>

In what ways are your five closest friends influencing you right now?

Are the people with whom you are spending time lifting you up or dragging you down?

Is there an area of your life that you want to change? With what type of people do you need to surround yourself to help make that change a reality?

27 EXPECT CHANGE(S)

"No man ever steps in the same river twice, for it's not the same river and he's not the same man."
        --Heraclitus

This quote resonates with me because it is a reminder that everything in life is constantly changing, including myself.

You may think to yourself, "Jamie, you must have every step in the Incline memorized, because you've done it so often." The fact of the matter is, the Incline is different each time I hike. The heavy volume of daily traffic changes the shape of each step constantly. This idea of constant change applies not only to the shape of the Incline, but also to the weather conditions that can turn a familiar hike into a new challenge at any movement. And as I reflected in the chapter "Expect the Unexpected," the weather can definitely change your experience on the Incline.

I remember one day when I did the Incline. When I started at the bottom, it was a bit overcast but a comfortable temperature, with no snow or ice. The path was clear. I was wearing running shoes and a light long-sleeved shirt.

I never imagined when I left my house that I'd be hiking in snow 30 minutes later, but I was.

It wasn't just frost. It was full-on snow coming down along with pellets of ice.

You can see from the picture, where the frost/snow line begins.

Sometimes as you are accomplishing your goals, the environment may become more hostile and unwelcoming. Just as the weather and environment can change quickly on the Incline, so to can the challenges we face as we work towards our goals.

Don't expect things to stay the same as you continue to grow and accomplish your goals. The environment in which you start your journey may be very different than the middle, and still different at the end.

Just as the steps of the Incline change regularly, you can't expect today's challenges to present themselves the same way as they did yesterday.

Just as the environment changes, you change too. Experiences change a person.

As you have new experiences and encounter new challenges it is important to reflect on them so that you can continue to grow and develop as an individual. We are never fully finished with our personal growth journey.

There is always more to learn, more challenges to overcome, and more opportunities to explore.

Caution: Don't expect everyone to understand what you have gone through or understand your experience. Similarly, don't expect them to recognize that you have grown into a different person.

Philippians 3:12 Not that I have already obtained all this, or have already arrived at my goal, but I press on to take hold of that for which Christ Jesus took hold of me.

1 Corinthians 13:11 *When I was a child, I spoke as a child, I understood as a child, I thought as a child: but when I became a man, I put away childish things.*

Personal Reflection:

Think about an experience in your life that changed you.

How was it that you changed and did others notice?

Have you ever had an experience where you changed the environment as a result of your experience?

How can you prepare for the changes in yourself and the changes in your environment as you achieve goals, finish projects or simply encounter life's obstacles?

28 DEVELOP RESILIENCE

Persistence in the face of difficulties or failures can lead to resilience.

Most of us, myself included, usually avoid uncomfortable situations or circumstances where failure might occur. However, it is often when finding ourselves in difficult situations or purposely doing hard things that we build resilience.

One of my two goals for the year was to finish the entire Incline in under 30 minutes. By that standard of measure, I failed nearly every time that I went out. If I were to focus on that alone, I probably would have become discouraged and quit. Instead, I tried to use any difficulties or failures as an opportunity to build resilience. Persistence and dedication are two key qualities that contribute to resilience, or the ability to bounce back from setbacks, challenges, and difficult situations. These qualities are not innate, but rather, they are developed and strengthened over time through practice and effort.

One way that persistence and dedication build resilience is

by helping us to persevere through difficult challenges and setbacks. When we are faced with obstacles such as an illness or a dislocated shoulder, it can be tempting to give up or become discouraged. However, by remaining persistent and dedicated to our goals and values, we can continue to push through these challenges and emerge stronger on the other side.

Another way that persistence and dedication contribute to resilience is by helping us to learn from our mistakes and failures. After failing or succeeding, look back at the journey—what went well, what didn't. Then ask yourself, "How can I improve the next time?"

When we make mistakes or encounter setbacks, it can be easy to become discouraged and give up. However, by remaining persistent and dedicated, we can use these experiences as opportunities to learn and grow, becoming more resilient in the process.

Resilience, like any other muscle, needs to be exercised in order to grow and strengthen. By doing hard things and remaining persistent and dedicated, we can build our resilience over time, becoming better equipped to handle whatever challenges come our way.

James 1:2-4 *Consider it pure joy, my brothers, when you are involved in various trials, because you know that the testing of your faith produces endurance. But you must let endurance have its full effect, so that you may be mature and complete, lacking nothing.*

2 Corinthians 4:8-9 *We are troubled on every side, yet not distressed; we are perplexed, but not in despair; Persecuted, but not forsaken; cast down, but not destroyed.*

Personal Reflections:

How are you building your resilience?

In what areas do you need to adopt a growth mindset?

29 GIVE IT YOUR **ALL**

When you are exhausted as you climb the Incline, your mind often tends to wander. As I strove to get faster each time, one of the puzzles that I tried to work out while climbing was "What is most important for me to focus on?" Or "What is my weakest link that I need to address in order to get better—or at least not fail?"

It was Vince Lombardi who said "Fatigue makes cowards of us all." When you are tired, what breaks down? How is your performance worse? Do you want to quit? How does conditioning and preparedness play a role? I've tried to do some pretty basic math in my head while doing the Incline—the fatigue and altitude make it nearly impossible to even think straight.

I identified what, for me, were the three most important components when tackling the Incline:

1. My head/heart—another way of looking at this is your will or your mind. Are you mentally tough enough to keep going? When you hit the wall, do you have grit and heart to push through?

2. My lungs. If you have never done aerobic exercise at 8000 ft above sea level, I will tell you that oxygen is scarce, and you can feel the struggle through your entire body. Often your lungs will burn and your head will throb. So, are my lungs the limiting factor? Is it the lack of oxygen that makes me want to slow down or quit?

3. Finally, my muscles—my legs. As I stated in the introduction, the average grade on the Incline is 45%. Taking steps for nearly a mile at a 45% upward angle quickly wears out the legs. If the muscles aren't there, it is a bitter experience. Sometime you wonder if you can lift your foot to the next step.

No matter how many times you do the Incline all three of these components play a part. I came to realize that it isn't necessarily any one component that was the limiting factor; it is all three. You must have a strong mind (or will), lungs, and strength all working in concert together. If you are lacking in any one, you will not have a peak performance.

That thought process reminded me of the two verses below.   If the "whole you"—heart, soul, mind, strength is not fully loving the Lord, you are missing out on His best for you.

Head, Lungs, Legs (*physical*): Heart, soul, strength (*spiritual*). Without all three in good shape, you will fail!

Mark 12:30   *Love the Lord your God with all your heart and with all your soul and with all your mind and with all your strength.*

Psalm 73:26 *My flesh and my heart may fail, but God is the strength of my heart and my portion forever.*

Personal Reflections:

Are all components operating at full capacity for you?

Which component is lacking and needs more attention?

What will you do about it?

30 STAY ON THE PATH

A previous chapter titled "Stay Focused" was a lesson about not letting your guard down when you believe that you have finished. This chapter deals more with staying focused on your goals and objectives as you work towards completion and work day in and day out in pursuit of your objectives.

On the Incline, there are many spots where you can wander a few feet off the steps to take a rest and enjoy a beautiful vista. Then there are trails that take you totally off of the Incline to another trail and to a completely different destination. Finally, there are locations on the trail where if you go off of the steps on either side, you are likely to tumble down a steep, rocky and dangerous precipice—resulting in severe bodily harm.

It's for this reason, that once you have established your goals and objectives, once you have analyzed the situation and developed a strategy and plan, once you have mapped out the route that you will take to arrive at your desired destination, you should STAY ON THE PATH.

I'm not saying not to be spontaneous or interruptible. I'm not suggesting that you shouldn't rest and enjoy the views along the way. I'm not saying that you shouldn't be adaptable to changing circumstances. But, I am saying that you need to stay focused on what you are there to do. Don't get distracted. Don't look for shortcuts. Don't chase the shiny objects that take you away from what you are pursuing.

In other aspects of life, just like on the Incline, there is plenty of room within the path to be spontaneous, to take rests, to meet with and engage other people. The danger occurs when you encounter and follow a distraction. Avoid getting sidetracked by new and exciting opportunities that may arise along the way. For instance, if the objective is to start a business and build it from scratch, chasing every new business idea or trend that comes along could lead to a lack of direction and focus.

If you are not crystal clear about what you are pursuing, why you are pursuing it or your priorities? You will be easily distracted and derailed by every seemingly promising opportunity or exciting new thing that comes your way. Or worse, you will actively seek out distractions that take you away from your objective.

Focus. Don't pay attention to distractions. Don't chase the shiny objects. Say "No." Stay on your path.

By saying no to distractions, you are saying yes to your priorities, yes to your goals, yes to your accomplishments, yes to your success. Staying on the right path requires evaluating every new opportunity and ensuring that it aligns with the established plan before pursuing it.

People may see the boundaries that you have set for yourself along the path you have chosen and criticize you for limiting yourself. Those boundaries aren't limiting, they are freeing—freeing you to accomplish what you want to accomplish and to live your life like you know it should be lived.

Proverbs 4:25-27 *Keep your eyes on the path, and look straight ahead. Make sure you are going the right way, and nothing will make you fall. Don't go to the right or to the left, and you will stay away from evil.*

Psalm 16:11 *You make known to me the path of life; in your presence there is fullness of joy; at your right hand are pleasures forevermore.*

Proverbs 14:12 *There is a way that seems right to a man, but its end is the way to death.*

Personal Reflections:

1. What are your distractions/weaknesses that you need to be aware of or eliminate?

2. Are you in the habit of saying "no" to requests, invitations, or distractions that are not aligned with your priorities and purpose?

31 FINISH STRONG!

One summer I received some unexpected feedback after holding a (summer) cadet leadership position at West Point. I was told that I had started off really strong. I was conscientious and focused, the best leader in the group. However, as time passed, I lost my focus, lost my energy and lost my drive. I finished ranked in the bottom half of the group that summer. My supervisor told me to start strong and finish strong. I received similar feedback a couple more times over the next few years—especially when it involved a long-term project or position.

As time passed, it finally sank in. I am now continuously conscious of the importance of finishing strong. This is related to the concept of consistency which I have discussed previously.

When hiking the Incline, I regularly see people who have stopped twenty or thirty steps from the top. They are gathering themselves or resting or something. I don't know. But they've stopped. It makes me think about stopping short of our goals or stopping when we are so close we can see the finish line.

Similarly, I also see people who start out really strong as I did that summer at West Point, but by the time they reach the last step, they are traveling at a snail's pace.

I don't say anything to either group of hikers except to encourage them because, hey, they are out there doing something hard.

But for me, and because of the lessons I learned early in my military career, I want to finish strong.

That is why my friend and I started running up the last thirty steps of Incline even though that is when we are most tired.

What did that do for me? I have found that finishing strong has had several benefits for me and likely for you too.

1. Finishing strong made me feel strong.

2. Finishing strong made me feel psychologically better for finishing a hard task on a positive note, giving me a sense of satisfaction.

3. Finishing strong demonstrated a commitment to excellence.

4. Finishing strong enhanced my reputation. People don't always see how you got there, but they often see how you finish. If you finish strong, they are going to notice. People are usually in disbelief when they see us running the last portion of the Incline.

Finish strong.

2 Timothy 4:7 *I have fought the good fight, I have finished the course, I have kept the faith.*

Ecclesiastes 7:8 *The end of the matter is better than it's beginning.*

2 Corinthians 8:11 *Now finish the work, so that your eager willingness to do it may be matched by your completion of it, according to your ability.*

My older son, Jonah, doing the Incline with me—running the final portion and finishing strong.

Personal Reflection:

Can you think of examples in your life where you have let down instead of finishing strong?

In what areas of your life do you need to make sure that you finish strong?

What will finishing strong do for you?

How do you finish strong spiritually?

32 EMBRACE HARD THINGS

You may have heard the phrase, "Your comfort zone is killing your potential." An underlying theme to this entire book and to the Incline challenge has been to seek out hard things, to deliberately seek discomfort.

Hard work and deliberate discomfort may not sound appealing at first, but they are both essential ingredients for success in any field. Whether you are a student, an athlete, or a professional, putting in the effort and seeking out discomfort can help you achieve your goals and fulfill your potential.

One of the reasons that I love doing the Incline is because there are no easy days on the Incline. Whether you have never done the Incline, done it once or done it one thousand times, the next time you do it, it will be hard and uncomfortable. As the saying goes, "The only easy day was yesterday!"

Despite the difficulty, I cannot think of a time when upon completion of the Incline that I did not feel good about what I had just accomplished. But also, there was always a sense of achievement and pride. Studies have shown that when we work hard and achieve something, our brains release a chemical called dopamine. This chemical is associated with feelings of pleasure and satisfaction; and it is often referred to as the "reward chemical." It is as if we were designed for hard work and achievement!

While it may seem counterintuitive, intentionally putting yourself in uncomfortable situations can help you grow and develop in ways you never thought possible. This can include pushing yourself physically by taking on a challenging workout routine or mentally by speaking in public or taking on a new job that stretches your abilities.

When you deliberately seek out discomfort, you also learn to embrace failure. Failure is an inevitable part of any journey towards success; it is important to view it as a learning opportunity rather than a setback. When you step outside of your comfort zone, you will inevitably face obstacles and setbacks. Viewing setbacks as opportunities for growth and learning can help you become more resilient and better equipped to face future challenges.

Finally, seeking out discomfort can also help you build confidence and resilience. When you push yourself to do things that scare you or make you uncomfortable, you prove to yourself that you are capable of more than you ever thought possible. As result, embracing discomfort can lead to increased confidence and the ability to tackle challenges with a newfound sense of courage and determination.

We were made to work hard and to do hard things. There is such a thing as "good tired."

When we do not work hard or do not push ourselves outside of our comfort zones, we may feel a sense of stagnation or even boredom. Without a sense of challenge and growth, we can become complacent and uninspired, which, in turn, can lead to a lack of motivation and a sense of dissatisfaction with our lives.

So . . . Always work hard, push yourself, and seek out challenges.

The Bible has much to say about the value and the necessity of working hard.

2 Chronicles 15:7 *But you, be strong and do not lose courage, for there is reward for your work.*

Proverbs 4:13 *All hard work brings a profit, but mere talk leads only to poverty.*

Galatians 6:9 *Let us not become weary in doing good, for at the proper time we will reap a harvest if we do not give up.*

2 Chronicles 15:7 *But you, take courage! Do not let your hands be weak, for your work shall be rewarded.*

Personal Reflection:

When was a time where discomfort in your life led to growth?

What is an area in your life right now where you are too comfortable and need to grow?

Think about a time where you worked hard to achieve a task and how you felt afterwards.

33 THE REST OF THE STORY

So, just a reminder of what started all of this— at the beginning of 2021, a friend of mine (West Point classmate) and I, both in our early 50s, in an effort to challenge ourselves, ward off old age and just as an excuse to spend some time together outdoors, set for ourselves two challenges:

1. Climb up the Manitou Incline in under 30 minutes.

2. Climb the Incline at least once a week all 52 weeks of the year.

All the previous chapters have been lessons learned in pursuit of those two goals.

So, how did it go? Well, you can see from my Strava app screenshot that on August 15, 2021, on a rainy Sunday evening, I hiked from Sign to Summit (first step to last) on the Manitou Incline in 29 minutes and 59 seconds— achieving my goal of under 30 minutes! I wish that I could say after that that it was easy and that I broke 30 minutes consistently. However, it did not get any easier, and I have not broken 30 minutes since—although I'm thinking of going for it again this year.

As for the second goal of doing the Incline at least once a week for a year, Yes, I achieved that goal! Through bad weather, being out of town, a dislocated and broken shoulder, COVID and a variety of other obstacles we continued to get out there every week. In fact, we still do it. We are now over two years past when we initially set our goals and we have continued into the second year of meeting weekly and doing the Incline together.

While the two goals mentioned above were always in the back of my mind; in this experience, it really *was* the journey that became important rather than the destination. We met and talked to so many people on the Incline. We became part of the community. We even earned Incline nicknames—The Apostles (James & John). We got outside and hiked every single week. We strengthened friendships. In a time when loneliness has reached epidemic proportions, we expanded our community. And as I've shared here, I also learned so much.

It may seem like this book has been about me, my friend, and our adventures. But really it has just been a vehicle to share lessons and truths that are true across time and life experiences.

I am not an extraordinary athlete or exceptionally driven. The goals that I set and accomplished which I have shared in this book are not world-class accomplishments. There were and are people on the Incline every single day who are faster than I am and who do way more Incline repetitions in a year than I could ever do.

The goals I set were for **me**. I knew they would push and challenge **me**.

But this book is really about **you**.

Life can be hard. Everyone (you) will face unexpected hardships.

None of us have arrived. None of us have achieved perfection. We can all improve and get better at whatever it is we are working towards.

Leaning on the lessons in this book and your answers to the personal reflections will carry you through.

Every day we live out self-fulling prophesies. One person may say, "There is no way that I will ever get any better," while another may say "I can definitely improve from where I am now."

Both people will likely end up being correct. On which side will you land?

So, what is your Manitou Incline? What do you want to accomplish? Walking up a bunch of stairs is such an appropriate metaphor for accomplishing goals or completing a project.

What is something in your life right now, big or small, that you need to "start climbing" and who can you get to help you "climb"?

Just try.

I could have looked up the Incline, made plans, set goals, had dreams etc., but if I never tried, I would likely still just be standing there admiring the challenge.

Take the first step.

The next right step, over and over again can accomplish more than you might think!

Enjoy the journey!

*At the top of the Incline with John

ABOUT THE AUTHOR

Jamie is a 1993 West Point graduate with a master's degree in psychology. After 26 years in the Army, Jamie now works for Young Life and also coaches transitioning veterans with The COMMIT Foundation. Jamie lives in Colorado Springs with his wife and three children.

Made in the USA
Las Vegas, NV
25 September 2024

95741114R00075